AF074521

AN IMPRINT OF WHAT BOOKS PRESS | LOS ANGELES

# THE SHOES OF OUR GUESTS

# THE SHOES OF OUR GUESTS

*Celeste Goyer*

Copyright © 2023 by Celeste Goyer. All rights reserved.
Published in the United States by Giant Claw,
an imprint of What Books Press, Los Angeles.

ISBN: 979-8-9866258-4-3

Library of Congress Control Number: 2023907841

Cover art: Gronk, *Home*, 2022
Book design by Ash Good, www.ashgood.com

Giant Claw
363 South Topanga Canyon Boulevard
Topanga, CA 90290

GIANTCLAWPRESS.COM

*for James Cushing
and Antoinette Sylvia Chaput*

## PROSE POEMS 2019-2021

### PART 1

| | |
|---|---|
| 7 | Deep Country Pastoral |
| 8 | Foreclosure Language |
| 9 | From My Mother's Camera (the plane flew on) |
| 10 | From the Ground Crew |
| 11 | Grownup Parties |
| 12 | Guesses with Hidden Parts |
| 13 | Here We Have to Eat Grass |
| 14 | High-Priced Climate |
| 15 | How Long Is Too Long |
| 16 | I'm Driving Slowly from the Wrong Place |
| 17 | In August My Name Leans Down |
| 18 | In the Hallway of Records |
| 19 | In the Lives of Half-Tamed Animals |
| 20 | In the Vault |
| 21 | Inflight Meals |
| 22 | Let's Get Lost |
| 23 | Madam Sphinx's Human Head |
| 24 | Missing in Hadley |
| 25 | Moving Day |
| 26 | Our Graduation Clock |
| 27 | Pink Petals Tied Together |
| 28 | The Same Old Footnote About the Rose Bush |

| | |
|---|---|
| 29 | A Secret Substance |
| 30 | Song About the Deer |
| 31 | Sounds for Wooden Chambers |
| 32 | Sugar Puff |
| 33 | Torn in the Middle |
| 34 | A Useful Pain Doll |
| 35 | With Whatever We Have Handy |
| 36 | A Womanly Chronology for Roasting |

PART 2

| | |
|---|---|
| 39 | Away from the Main Road |
| 40 | A Bucket for Peace |
| 41 | Emergency Pull Toy Dissertation |
| 42 | From the Citizen's Almanac |
| 43 | Hidden Entrance |
| 44 | A Human Dream Standing on One Foot |
| 45 | I'm a Useless, Trivial Hairball |
| 46 | Kanji Speak to Me |
| 47 | A Kind of Mercury the Weather Only Ruins |
| 48 | Movies About Sin and Whatever That Means |
| 49 | A Nervous Case of Family Romance |
| 50 | The New Lightweight Eggs |
| 51 | Oh, Spring, That's All |
| 52 | On the Real Seabed |
| 53 | One Dress Divided Into Armor (and the bats flew in) |

| | |
|---|---|
| 54 | Pictures of Birds |
| 55 | Reaching This Place |
| 56 | Resurrection Symphony |
| 57 | Royal Stains |
| 58 | The Sitting Voice |
| 59 | Summer's Gift Cake |
| 60 | Swimmers Full of Sunshine |
| 61 | Taped to a Piano |
| 62 | What Dreams Learn About Us |
| 63 | What Just Happened |
| 64 | The Whole Horse, Not Just the Head |
| 65 | Why That Darling |
| 66 | Winter Wheat |
| 67 | You Can Finish This Without Me |
| 68 | Your Spider Knows |
| | |
| 71 | Acknowledgments |

# PART 1

> Now there is this gulping ceremony with my mother, this hand-shaking ceremony with my father; now I must go on waving, I must go on waving, till we turn the corner.
>
> —Virginia Woolf
> *The Waves*

# DEEP COUNTRY PASTORAL

Our train, our city clothes—it hurt to bury them. Now our life's asleep on one green pinpoint. We are human shovels, rakes, hoes. We dig to keep from being buried.

We were told morning light has the key that bears fruit, so we keep looking for it, rising earlier each day. All afternoon the grass grows, more than ten horses can eat. We shave the new calves, pick blackberries. It's a long, long day with an expiration date and a realtor's phone number hidden in it.

The irony of this kind of burial couldn't crack our back-to-the-land mothers. They'd learned the secret of the homemade egg: inside is a water droplet with another goal, beautiful and powerful. This is how we speak here, the way we'd tell a dream to someone half-listening, someone in a heat trance concentrating on their melting popsicle, or watching out the bay window a yellow cat crouching, about to jump up onto the mailbox.

# FORECLOSURE LANGUAGE

*for Isabel Goyer*

They're auctioning an idea this morning outside the front doors of the Chino branch of the San Bernardino Public Library. There's a trash can, two slatted benches and a rectangle of shade. The sign letters on the building are in Times New Roman. A few people stand silently as a man reads from a clipboard. It seems very long, and the sun climbs. He's reading us to sleep.

The bidders, or witnesses—who are they? They look as solemn as we feel. Wouldn't they rather be walking through the park on their way to a nice breakfast? They have our uncle's paratrooper eyes.

Finally the man reaches our number on the list, and we recognize our own ghosts, their soft, silly faces, never far from us. We suddenly feel a little protective of the stagnant pool water, the places where the roof leaked into the dining room, and the skinny tree where Renee sat with her dog and smoked. Who is to say the roaches baked into the puddled oil on the garage floor like dark, rainbowed diadems were not also rightful children?

Someone throws one coin, then two. We expected no better, but somehow it's impossible now to imagine the winning bidder opening the right side of the front double door. We'd have to hear again the scrape of the brass against the brown tile. We thought we killed them both—the metal scrape of the brass and the sharp squeak of the hinges. And the worn carpet with the tacks sticking up—how could we have left it lying in wait? We take him aside after he signs, shake his hand, and you, my sister, whisper the word 'fire' into his ear.

# FROM MY MOTHER'S CAMERA (THE PLANE FLEW ON)

See me in my spinning dress with one dead bird and one live one, secrets hidden in my expression like stones in a handkerchief. There I am kneeling in the barn wrapping French bread in fresh plaster. Trying to change what you don't understand in your children just creates new people you don't understand.

I was eight years old when my mother was arrested smuggling pomegranates to Athens under her black fur coat. Here she is wearing a white scarf over her hair, sleek and squinting as a seal. Under her coat the regal pomegranates rest gently, according to the stars. "I was loved and not loved," she said, "and I was scared of both." The worms in the field hide inside the spider, it is said.

Now here's my father, rowing a boat full of ink across a river, his mouth level, even with the horizon. The man is of the house, the woman of the cellar, forever lying underneath.

# FROM THE GROUND CREW

Our family rented birds in the Mojave Desert to help with the strong wind. My brother called for help: "They are everywhere—rude, bad-tempered, unfriendly!" He ran and caught some, but it didn't end there.

I should have a warm feeling about the air, but I feel only a warning of something, a forgetfulness from all sides. I'm frosty, frigid despite the heat.

And Lord, a man with wings over six-hundred-feet wide stands above me, looking down through the solar system. He's *that* man, the man who emptied the dining room of oxygen. How long will it be before noon's circle sweeps him off my desk? I'm holding my breath here. I have 3500 liters saved up, as of last night.

# GROWNUP PARTIES

By 11 o'clock that guy has offended just about everyone and the bacteria level's off the charts in the stuffed clams. Half the party's in the kitchen and the other half's trying to talk over Herb Alpert and the Tijuana Brass.

Just before midnight, the hosts bring out their tiniest children to MC the departure ritual. "How sweeeet," we say, spilling our drinks. But it's 12:20 now, the porch's birthday. "Oh, honey," we say, sending the little true things back up to bed, above the smoke and littered lobster shells, the bourbon smog bank settled in the white and gold living room.

# GUESSES WITH HIDDEN PARTS

Back when she believed that everything that was fine was easy, Mother placed a mirror in the cupboard with her copy of *The Book of Everything*, full of instructions and warnings in other languages. She found white rope and tied on her wings with eyes closed, loosening the knots so she could wear them walking around. We understand such love.

In her brightly colored dress, flashlight, and a voice from under the snow, she spoke as if in front of a camera, letting the light shake her in its shadows. She tried to look as she did before this short film impressed its images on her moist, closed eyes.

# HERE WE HAVE TO EAT GRASS

Lovers and devotees waited on shore, hoping for fur hats from the wreck, but nothing was found in the rooms of the old, old ship but blue shadows. The absurd pride of such hats is real, the ease of connection one feels wearing them, even though the head is sweating. For once, you are not alone, whatever the cost. I remember a brown bear pointing to the waves. "I was the last one of my father's sons to live a bear's life," he said. "Here my sons have to eat grass."

The lovers had many stories and many job titles. I heard them all, waiting there in the thin layers of morning. They come back to me, like white snow on a white door.

# HIGH-PRICED CLIMATE

The cheerful-looking hermit thrush hopped into the weeds out of sight to find a little heap of soil cursed by her father, a hopeless old earthquake with rear-facing wings. What could have possessed her to stop so long on his hollow island? Her spotted breast had an allergy to the soles of heavy shoes, to chariot wheels. The hermit thrush's strength also worked to hold other things in place—a kind of slow-motion self-homicide by kinship, the fine art of composing a costume for sloping shoulders before they can put their armor on.

# HOW LONG IS TOO LONG

Dust loves its job filling holes. Ants dig it out again to clear their highways and halls. I'm suspended in this heat like a bubble in molten glass. My bed's black, my clothes and books only stay inflated with cool air pumps. I sit on the bed and look at them. "I can talk like anybody else," I say, but I don't hear anything come out.

Around noon, the wind purses its lips for the afternoon blow. A whole lot of sand needs a change of scenery. The heat makes us move deliberately, like monks at our tasks with ritual hands.

I've read about rivers and how to use them, so this year I'm rebuilding my bridges to look more like shoes. The true power of a little water finding its way.

# I'M DRIVING SLOWLY FROM THE WRONG PLACE

In the depths of enemy territory (the high school parking lot), I dug a hole in the ground for the disquieting state of things and the friendly gesture that deflowers girls in hallways with its wooden teeth. I found my classmate, a socially prominent boy, weeping on a chair after the play. I put my arm around him on that summer night. For hours we sat destroying the correct answers, twenty thousand of them. We put on an unforgettable show!

Now the word 'small' reappears and talks to me. It moves and it glides with its unseen body between me and the light through the bamboo. We are trying to decide if we can be friends. The whole city's pitching in to take a good look.

# IN AUGUST MY NAME LEANS DOWN

My name's just one of millions, official rephrasings of a death that gleams.

The new me must be adequate and continuous, the shoes I will wear in these green hills, official gear for riding against ghosts and feeding this large family full of children who need to know the reasons for things. And who will keep the men under control, clean up their buttery chins when August falls downstairs suddenly, chipping a tooth?

I'm older now—I can swim toward any shore I can see without my glasses. Come sing pizzicato with me. Our afternoons together will be dark and beautiful, full of armchairs we have loved, rolling chairs that hosted our theatricals. We'll warm the air with our coiled blood. Birth and shopping are gaining on us. I can't afford a thunderstorm but I'll order one anyway.

# IN THE HALLWAY OF RECORDS

Waiting in line, I examine my inability to wait completely, with true commitment to indefinite delay. This talent for waiting is what ants have instead of hearts. The record keepers say, "Each great person has an ant waiting to carry their corpse away in its jaws."

Outside, mountains erode visibly, like pyramids made of down escalators. I see my friends up there—tiny specks. Down here, I defend my territory while I've got it, sprinkle the corners with salt, lime, and soda. The rocks say, "Don't make me crush you." I live in hope of never knowing the inner lives of things, the mountain and planet names used to curse me.

# IN THE LIVES OF HALF-TAMED ANIMALS

The practice of teaching humility to pine cones—I'm interested in it. Because there's my dad, wrapping a spiral ham in black cloth. It puts a strain on a person.

# IN THE VAULT

I kept it in a quiet box for you—the phone's ring that you didn't answer, the Easter clothes your mother wore until they collapsed, your favorite drop, the terrible drop, the years when you did nothing.

I kept it for you—the beauty parlor, the mink coat, the green lines on the little squirrel you wanted, your whisky auto parts and what they saw, the five minutes you shouldn't have been wearing your suede gloves, that look on the boy's face.

I kept it in the freezer for you—the noise you make in bed when things are delayed, when there's no wind, the princess dress roller skating down a dark street, the anonymous tip from the parking attendant.

I kept it safe for you—the open sea, how you shouted when you collided with it, the deep sugar where your good man died—the nasty creaking in front of your house in winter.

I buried it for you—the hat that fell in front of your car, how the wheels sounded.

# INFLIGHT MEALS

I believe if I spill my milk enough times my mother will tell the story again, how she tried to back out on her wedding day, and her mother said, "That's nice, dear. Now put your dress on."

Our volatile Dad's made of polyester, creases built-in at the airplane factory. Obsidian buttons hold his face on tight, make cold fire we all duck from during dinners. We ordered a cotton Dad, but they won't come into style for another ten years. He's better off in his buzzing box that hangs in the sky, one hand on the throttle, one on the control stick between his legs, manipulating the ailerons, the elevators.

Mom's a volunteer chemist here on loan from Corning, where glass lids are born. She's white, soft, folded carefully in many pieces, each piece with its own French name that we kiss.

# LET'S GET LOST

I'll need a mother's sentences to protect my story from harm, my story of women getting lost in their relationships. I'll need words with more hands, like tree branches.

Families, no matter how loving, need a back door. As we see the huge world gather around us, we rush to slip free of caution. We drop the family map and fall into the opening where the woman's character is born—that *terra incognita*.

I was in the dark, on the sidelines, but proud of my life. I'd picked up this map one wet and freezing day to prove that women don't have to disappear into calm, decorated photographs. I woke up as a couple, taking root in the trunk of someone else's car, leaning backwards. It's true, women in relationships disappear like fruits into the swollen questions where they live, wondering how they came into this composition, then looking to disappear again, with many a squirmy official break and camouflage jumpsuit lying down on wrong-way tracks.

I woke up with a handful of false starts but no lines of my own. You might say I was a Christmas cold, traveling into relationships like fruit into ghastly brand-new kitchens, photographed but never still. I cheated a lot at first with various border huts in the snow (it was in fact rubble made of ice) until early morning spilled its guts. My excuses stepped back. It was an early morning step-back world in someone else's car where the passenger, hopeful but ultimately silent, rides alone.

# MADAM SPHINX'S HUMAN HEAD

Tonight's a kind of blanket knitted from old radio, where the darkness in the darkness is made. The sun's dark too, with a built-in heaven. In my unrealistic dreaming, a bird will soon take that old disease away.

One of our relatives flies to the sun in a huge pale blue robe. The book of the 20th century was not for him. If like him we follow our own ideas, will we find new muscles, or just new nails? Maybe flames in golden corners were a poor partner choice, but our leader says, at least there's a lot of light from a moon without skin, a moon that lives alone in real life.

Hopefully this night doesn't need me to wait much longer, standing out here in the damp on my one leg of bread. Do your best, our leader says.

# MISSING IN HADLEY

The woman living in my refrigerator, maybe my sister, makes me choose between butter and a new synthetic version when I open the door. Apologizing for the age of the leftovers, I run out.

The next time I see her, my sister's a leaf-shaped piece of maple sugar candy. Her husband's fine with it, even though she's a little stale and smells like our aunt's scarf drawer. After forty years with a river in her basement, she's as perky as ever. Those two are the only couple I know still having sex, so let's not blame marriage for everything.

Leave a cloud bank in the back of the fridge long enough and the mold will give it the look of distant mountains. I've decided there's something majestic about our wrinkles, the way they catch and hold the snow.

# MOVING DAY

On moving day, we wake early to make our mark in the big book, and what wisdom we once claimed runs invisibly out of our hands. Carrying our boxes like ants moving over the blank parts of drawings, we follow the great avenues. We turn back on ourselves many times on moving day like old rivers, like brown cats in hallways.

They can be very destructive, these movements beyond our reach. We tie our shoes into sets of two, name them twins and set them on their roads.

# OUR GRADUATION CLOCK

My neighbor's been growing sea legs. Each earthquake she walks a little steadier. Her old man up the canyon rumbles on with his promises of cracks opening up in the good old days to come. She texts me, "Do twin beds pushed together really make a king?" I text her back, "Not for long."

Winter light slides into our yards, each leaf lit up sideways, even the blighted ones. They're singing in yellow-green. I collect some tools to loan her. A chisel for her pocket, a diving suit and helmet to wear, as nodding she'll agree with him, "Yes, all you say is true," then over the side of the rowboat she'll step, into tossing darkness.

# PINK PETALS TIED TOGETHER

The girl kept looking for the hidden magnet that made everyone jump. She wouldn't go home until it was safe, until lilac season wrapped the porches. She wouldn't go home until her sister and brother appeared as people again, came down from the attic where they lived rolled up, soft and silent as old quilts.

She wanted her friends to come to her place to eat, find what was hidden in the sugar bowl, an agenda written to protect all dining rooms from warfare. Her fingers, she believed, corresponded in Japanese to 'pink petals tied together.' She quietly dreamed in owl language of a pony with horns and an old blanket. She'd spend the summer under her sister's bouffant hair. Her sister's dark nails, her lips salty and furious.

# THE SAME OLD FOOTNOTE ABOUT THE ROSE BUSH

At the back of your garden, the grass wore a loose, embarrassed look, full of forgotten objects. "I need you," they called, too far away to be heard. A close relative cut off his bloody tail, kept it in an old newspaper. It's normal in your family. Parts of the old body are removed by the sick. Close friendships form, then the wind eats them, plants clover and grass. Creating a quiet island requires a lot of skill. Beneath it, dry skin awaits the hammer.

Who doesn't think they paid to be satisfied? You tried to pay a small amount in pine needles to your specialist after twelve years in therapy. You accepted a dream from him about an old woman and then didn't dream it. Quiet! Be careful! At the end of each page waits her old pink name!

# A SECRET SUBSTANCE

A man opened a capsule, extracted a small, metallic object he could rely on month after month, season after season. He placed it in a drawer. Outside his window, the land in its strange mountain dress ate a glass of ice, and snow dove down from a great height. He knows he's locked in a big hole and this sad story hardens his tongue, burned to the point of extinction. If you feed a beast on broken plates, expect to bury it.

One side of his desk was called 'down' and the other side was called 'damn.' Another page titled 'unrest' he filed in a fourth category called 'disagreements.' On this page, my first and his last name were combined.

# SONG ABOUT THE DEER

In this narrow, powder-soft library, we spend our lunch money nervously on white cloth napkins, a pair of scissors. We're learning to act, to sing, vivacious beginners who hope no one notices when we fall from the stove to the table. It's not a novelette. But who can say?

On a snowy roof, our teacher lifts his greatcoat, releasing the gorgeous owls. But the last handful, so much quieter, sit protected in their sleepy nursery. They feed on our insecurity in an orderly yet kind way. The body, all we really have in our cross-legged circle, maps out our odd or even future. I'm shaking like a lilac begging with a softshoe breath. The mates our sweaters lost wait behind furniture, their cobwebbed arms waving in the warm furnace currents.

I fell behind in the song about the deer as we glued our masks into dark triangle noses, and everywhere my limbs, my tongue.

# SOUNDS FOR WOODEN CHAMBERS

In the hills, dust from the fire fell and last night's moonlight came back like there was purpose in it. I was tied to the ground in matching pajamas as music filled the whole atmosphere.

This summer we exchanged cakes, tied ropes to the furniture to guide us through rooms. There's always a spirit coming in here that's the size of a house—when it arrives, you are trapped watching wooden shepherds pointing sticks at unmarked children. But listen, a wheat field's busy kneeling in my bathtub—so shouldn't we try to stay, build a relationship with leaves? Your peeling machines will take millions of years yet, and we still have corn, these bright colors stuck to us, this little music, this tall, swinging air.

# SUGAR PUFF

Dad walks around the garden like someone with cold metal in his mouth, as light swirls in summertime's blue sky. He can't predict who also waits in his mouth's darkness and who will speak first.

Sugar Puff, the world's oldest pony, wants to beat him up for treating kids the way he does. Sugar Puff does beat him up, while we watch. Then he grows depressed, knowing the beatings do no good and the letter 'O' is just another sort of bathtub where we can lose our good watches, unchanged in shape since the sun appeared on the back of yesterday's money. Dad gets a flashlight to lead the way to his happy and exciting life, a flame tattooed around his mouth.

# TORN IN THE MIDDLE

Before summer was out at our rented farmhouse, something maple-colored crawled under the fridge, then slumped alone into a soft gray shape, like a blurred handbag. The house was full of its transparent presence. Think about it—people hurt those who fall. Our mistakes are ancient, completely unoriginal. Our last hour will be spent in yawning.

We drove away silently, the car's trunk stuffed with the word 'no' growing larger and larger in the heat.

# A USEFUL PAIN DOLL

For six years my neighbor's wife has been reading aloud from *The Old Mountain Book* and I can hear every word through the walls. Some chapters are useful, such as when the main character throws a straw hat full of holes into a river and never speaks of it again. I can relate. I've spent most of the winters since 2012 out of this world, making conversation with a person under the ground. That's enough.

# WITH WHATEVER WE HAVE HANDY

Because she went away into the dusty dunes where the beach plums grow, I now connect with my mother only on long phone calls that trail off at the end.

We are the seven baby teeth she swallowed. We grew in her stomach—golden grain in golden fields eaten by golden finches who eat so much they explode like small sunbursts. My mother cries for her blue Shirley Temple drinking glass as she tends to do when she's tired or has a cold. I don't know why she died.

Oh, my colored pencils, you sing and I can't hear you now. After too many leaky promises, finally I ended up naked, asking, "What can I actually see from down here?" and the more I asked the less I wanted to wait around to find out.

# A WOMANLY CHRONOLOGY FOR ROASTING

I'm grateful for enchanted love's periodic transfer, the way it bleeds big answers onto our most aromatic questions. I asked you to help me rebel against myself, but that was a disaster. 'Fish or cut bait,' the motto carved on our childhood bed, had a short shelf life, ended our love affair with a single piece of clothing.

I begged you to contradict me, save me from the dire sort of respect that once burned a bare patch onto my head. It feels like a long time ago, yet also far off in the future, this light, its iron content. Remember when such words confused us with their bouncy spin and confining narrative? Yes, in California our skin feels different. The correct answer was sent to us by your smile, your good cheer like old wax rattling in a box.

Sticky notes of the elderly take on a futuristic, knowing air, leaving our own words in ruins. I protest their lack of light, their dried fish in chains.

# PART 2

"What," I asked Cage, "is the advantage of not knowing what you are doing?" "It cheers up the knowing," he explained. "Otherwise, knowing will be very self-conscious and frequently guilty."

—John Ashbery
*Reported Sightings: Art Chronicles 1957-1987*

# AWAY FROM THE MAIN ROAD

The lion behind us believes in us—at least he wants to wear our shoes, our gloves. He had thin-pressed lips even before birth, and a nervous system of hard ice, with those old-fashioned green eyes that can follow the faintest trail. My dream last night placed him on a cold sidewalk, about to drag his chain across a quiet, empty street. Horses made of dense cake lay down to wait, stretched out between the shafts of carriages. Their dark, square-cut heads weighed as much as pianos.

And because this hell went up quickly and convincingly, a small crowd gathered to keep their most ethereal longings warm, that the lion then immediately plowed down.

# A BUCKET FOR PEACE

What are we doing here? Just talking, friend. The rattan shell is broken on your left shoulder, the train wears its fedora. You see? We are two, you old monkey, just say yes to everything—work with me.

A few boxes full of mushrooms and leaves, some serious legs, but are you free? Good people, you have those names. You are not married but you have sinned again. Sorry. You did it. Please don't throw it away. I'll throw it away. Your self-governed divorce city is closed. Did you choose butter? I have bark, a mouth as deep as a road. We are very different. You can simply tell us different things about love.

# EMERGENCY PULL TOY DISSERTATION

We're making Sundays mobile to roll through the tough countryside gluing our people's collapse back together with the sound of pipers. It's a career that nobody talks you through. The most important thing we've saved so far was a drawing of a farmer cutting a stone in half that couldn't be eaten whole.

It's crazy, I guess, to think we can forget where and when the disaster was inserted. Now we're as old as our ship was when the instructions were lost. Monday hides a basket of soot in its big dark hoof, or so Papa hinted on the night he died. Still, do we need to be constantly on the lookout, take everything with us whenever we leave?

If only our beautiful milk cow would share her solid gold eyelashes, we could ride to the top of summer's haystack, braid permanent crowns for the young mothers.

# FROM THE CITIZEN'S ALMANAC

The season's almost over, so let's take a farewell tour today. We'll go slowly in our white coats, with our damn grace and our credentials—small pieces of paper on which is written 'nice suit,' and 'it all makes sense.' What should I do to sleep tonight? The village calendar looks like a donkey on my desk. I jump a mile when I see summer returning to the suburbs in an orange homemade tent. I waited all day for your thumbprint dress to walk by and give me a list of your favorite activities.

The city's poem sounds like a waterspout in my closet. How can I stay awake when I feel so rejected? If I quickly put on my dark sweatshirt and stumble into my minimum wage job downstairs sweeping up pine needles, maybe no one will notice that there's nothing at all written on them.

# HIDDEN ENTRANCE

Today Lake Otsego establishes summer. She rises from her bed this morning to row a submerged boat on her wide blue flank, her private hills of glass below. A man shouts, "My dear, it's time for love."

Two women murmur as they float, making a basket for lost ducks. Lifeguards climb up on the dock, sunken boats cool in their hands. The rules they ask us to follow are written with gold stripes and blue-edged shadows on leaves of yellow plants.

# A HUMAN DREAM STANDING ON ONE FOOT

We are permanent audience, we've forgotten how to do it ourselves, how to grow from the inside. We shrug, "You see? This is all. It must be enough." I have strength left in my arms, but who will buy it? Who will buy me? Maybe all I gave away is all I have to offer. I once had a yellow cardboard box complete with a yellow hole, something more 'me' than you'll ever know. What I exchanged for it was not worth it—my lungs, my ears, my open throat, back when they were new. There are those who would probably buy me now even without a mask, before I expire from my injuries.

My dream is the human dream of the Gulf Coast standing on one foot. I grow larger, more solid, hold out my arms to people and audiences, revealing my empty black box close up, for the birth, for whatever's needed, a flag with a spoon filled with a white square hole.

# I'M A USELESS, TRIVIAL HAIRBALL

I like to cook, I like hanging suspended in the shade of tall trees, writing on bread. I admit I'm a loser of this world, I'm part of it, I live here on a rock (stolen), doing nothing for my beans and peas. The roof of the house is a tender bright green color and I'm doing nothing to protect it from oxidation, from autumn, from birds, from the coming snow. If anyone finds this, tell them I'm sorry, I wanted to help.

I'm no good. I can't improve anything. I live here with the words 'a great traitor' sewn on my shirts. Why can't I stop the four-hundred-pound bear from moving into the kitchen, the hot tub? I can't concentrate while you're nailing your hats to the walls, so I'm writing this letter in the oven on bread, scratching words on it with a tiny needle.

Yes, I'm sick, I'm part of the entire problem of sickness. I have a big key to this rock (stolen), with the words 'pretending everything's okay' on it, a motto I can't escape. Is this proof I'm actually already dead?

My head aches as I sew nightgowns and write letters in the oven. I can handle anything except the coming hard years but still I want to help. I'm stating this as plainly as I can stand to under these conditions, hoping for some understanding one day. I destroyed this place, I am part of it, I can't prove that everything's fine. Good food's everywhere except in the right kitchens. I hear you clearly with my remaining good ear.

# KANJI SPEAK TO ME

I'm traveling to Japan on a bicycle powered by rainwater. It will take four weeks to get there. My rucksack holds rice, fish, tea. I am a woman running from a small man with an airplane. The sun over the mountain's too big to eat.

I'm leaving Tokyo tonight in an electric car delivering sushi. I've had too many alcohol—three too many —to go far. It will take seven hours for the fire to go out in the rice field and two years to forget what that woman said to me. I am a small fish from a rainy river. Too small to eat.

Osaka authorities asked me to come and speak about meat. I'm allowing three weeks to write my speech, five minutes to deliver it. I'd rather be climbing a big mountain with tea and rice in a rucksack. Too few bicycles, not enough sun.

On Hokkaido, men wrap women in three strands of barbed wire before going out to work in the morning. They generate electricity by wrapping fish in rice. Sun over the river means no rain tomorrow.

# A KIND OF MERCURY THAT WEATHER ONLY RUINS

An enormous mudslide declares that the female brain is smoother, its cravings more superficial. Every wandering clock ignores her. Her bite-sized confessions come out spasmodic and cloudy. Whereas in man the crowd is his rhythm. With woman, the swing element is part of her whole shape, clearly recognizable like paint in soup.

A man's success comes in waves of public explosions. A woman's body is a shy spoon, the debt of her organs, their comfortable furniture separated by ropes.

# MOVIES ABOUT SIN AND WHATEVER THAT MEANS

Jane came in from the sidewalk with her small mouth. She whispered, "Men follow me with gloves and give me dust—here it is. Take some." Who wants such questions and promises? Who wants to wipe that taste from their mouth?

We stayed for one more drink anyway to watch Mrs. Braddock dancing who used to be my friend. Later we went to the next place, stumping along to say how do you do, and when I came back to the bar, the unique house that we built had been lost. Who cares. When you tell a machine to do something twice, it's as though you never asked it at all.

Jane grabbed my arm. An army officer once taught her how to want the partners you don't have by dancing with them. Would I ever find someone who wouldn't play carelessly with my parts? Who'd show me how to take this all in, how to dance on tables with my heavy hips, make inviting circles with my fingers and bow when the song ends? Jane too had been turned around too many times in life. When she sang to me, sad and charming shadows floated down outside. "Let's go have a look," she said, so many times.

This is for the painful list of topics she brought from Chicago to New York. This is for the stuffed donkey that's neither boy nor girl, father nor mother. "Listen," she said, "the cognac's not good."

# A NERVOUS CASE OF
# FAMILY ROMANCE

You went to bed with Hart Crane this morning just as New York was going to bed with Mexico after walking all night in the rain. "You have to teach your parents to drink and be angry with you," you said. The umbrella tried, with touching and doomed efforts, to keep you dry.

You tried going to bed with the theater next. It was full of thirst and earnest advice to write more letters to your mother. Your self-explanations woke up instead, barking like hysterical dogs. Your uncomprehending father honored you by slowing his car to stare at you on the street, the curse of ugly parentage on your shoulders. This finally proved too much for you to sleep through.

You tipped the scales in the other direction then and went to bed with an ogre to redress the balance of your lonely birthright. "I made no demands," you insisted, as the dream university filled your shoes with sand, planted them like seeds.

# THE NEW LIGHTWEIGHT EGGS

Tonight's moon wears yellow tulle and carries a prop sword before her bosom, guarding our sleepiness. I'm vaguely jealous to see my evening dresses walking about the garden without me, measuring for flower beds and gazebos with those unfolding wooden yardsticks.

I remember how happy you were when you discovered the bridge they sent you by mistake. You buried the old man under it on New Year's Day in 1979. Four new worlds started slowly spinning then, and as they turned, their shiny petals opened. One old world expired with a groan in its own muddy branches. You never spoke its name again.

It's just dark enough to make out the pinhole view of Raymond Chandler's final bedroom floating on the wall above your desk, covered as it is with crumpled Beethoven sonatas. He realized there were questions we really don't want to answer, such as 'Do you want this job or not?' At midnight, the rocking motion of your chair slowly stops. Fog, shaky and soft, repairs such parts as it can before sunrise.

On the wooden stairs, my tiny horses stomp up to bed. We return to where we love, what we love. Twenty-two episodes will tell the story.

# OH, SPRING, THAT'S ALL

At this point in the play the room's full of bronzed leaves and copper blue water. When two women wrapped in sweaters enter to sharpen pencils, we are thrilled. "They are pointed sticks," says the older one. Ah, ah, it's all clear. They're making a small fire in the bottom of a burnt hole. They're dreaming of the tiny factories down there where feathers are singed going up in smoke. In the balcony, we lie down and wait for the next act to make small V-shaped creases on our thighs.

The younger woman burns her workbook and its hidden message is lost: *Say hello to the winners in their dirty boat—but don't enter their world. We will shine on—oh spring—on everything.*

A hard-fighting woman shines; she never throws away emotions on vast gold eggs and on men contaminated with raw materials. Find gold, find gold's confusion. The next big fight? We know it's not far away.

# ON THE REAL SEABED

For a sponge bath on a recreated Japanese island, my girl brought along eight animals to hold up her hair as she bathed. Like her, one day you'll wake up, begin to develop an egg, and do what you need. A new cycle is always right. Why don't you play your role? Your sound is thunder and lightning, the wind.

In her tub she washes the mountains with poured water. A storm begins to accumulate—blood pressure's full with dew. Everything on earth comes from her hip, the left eye of the sun, and the eye of the moon. We'll drink the world again to start it anew. Shiva will decide what remains, then heaven and earth will, for the first time, unite. They'll walk with us into the world, clean golden butter holding up its roof. We'll remain in our boots with our feet in the mountains.

Vishnu sleeps; Brahma's neck appears as a lotus. That's where we'll marry. I can't say anything better.

# ONE DRESS DIVIDED INTO ARMOR (AND THE BATS FLEW IN)

Under the bridge where your sentence waits, the goddess of cold rain, of modern clouds, prepares to bring forth roses. It's late in the winter. Birds beat up other birds for singing their songs. That may seem strange if you're not used to it.

All of you, you have ropes too, and bags filled with flour. The more the natural heart descends, the higher it will sink. Into this golden circle I'll set the sun. Feel how it works, how everyone laughs. Walk, walk, nothing goes far. God is green, made of the way beets smell cooking. The flowers will find their way back to blooming. Papier mâché babies, we see you there in the choir!

I'll stay up all night in a remnant of forest filling a blanket with what I know. Duck shadow, human symbol, what am I? I am the ghost daughter of my lost fire. I've seen you under lamplight, my chosen, are you spirit? Paris is under a heavy choke chain, goddamnit, she's frozen, so make it snow. Let me remember, oh ghost of a fever that crossed my lips, let me spit once. Where are you? The old train has gone too far away. It may be some time before I can speak of its path under the stars, its shadows walking a thin plank.

In Stravinsky's dream, a black horse put soup on the table, and rolls, and a hive for honey, suggesting a deep jewelry gleaming. The tea was ringing like a gong, like a ditty, like a scrawny cry, like deer going by through the goldenrod.

We must do what we can, by burning it first. This is not the beginning—this is a reckoning. No one can drive this car.

# PICTURES OF BIRDS

Here we are again, at work in the morning on our pictures of birds. I drove to the usual places, I said 'hi' to everyone, forgetting what happened last year—the year of glass faces.

A peculiar silent flatness arrived on February 19th. As you will see I did not find many birds on this trip. I got up at 2:30, but most of the geese and cranes had already flown north. No one was there on the lake, cold and salty as desire. My photos from this trip are finicky, oddly impersonal. Another morning of working, hoping that all will be well. In this way I move without any movement. Here is a photo of the last bird.

# REACHING THIS PLACE

Much has been written about dust, about the way horses laugh at us, at our feelings. We need people from sunken ships, but for what, we don't know.

I've always raised children from flour, read to them with glowing tongue. Babies tried to teach me, but I only learned a few words. For instance, 'blue fence' means the pattern of a flower compatible with the sun, or a bird traveling back and forth on a ferryboat. Babies too expand their wings before flying. We need a sunken ship because it knows how to look for something else. And now my foolish actions must get to work.

# RESURRECTION SYMPHONY

Our wandering Lazarus buttonholes me in the hallway. He's writing a book about the indifferent care of the newly dead—the terrible injustice. It's not an earthquake that shakes the mattress and sends him jumping, but his belief in a fallen world. I agree that everything's alive, but the line must be drawn somewhere regarding what gets to move around.

Let's visit Mahler this lovely autumn day. "Mmmmm, yes," he says, as he stacks a cart full of stolen goods, ears cocked for the hymns of conjugating whales. "Believe…believe….cease thy trembling, prepare thyself for life," he murmurs, trying on our sweaters in the afternoon sun.

# ROYAL STAINS

*for Holaday Mason*

Scissors, where are you? My hair's standing on end in one clotted hank. It wants convincing that we're cared about. While we wait, it's taken up felting mice, weaving them tightly to my neck. I'm sure it was our shared blanket like a thick dust devil that tangled my hair, turning knots into a competition only a decision expert (such as a knife) could win.

Anyone can press their thumb on a nail and make a red seed, yet even this jewel will sink when blood spills in the throat itself. You owe me a birthday gift of a hair-brushing and a pomegranate. Many things are too heavy to carry. They must be worn.

# THE SITTING VOICE

Those I cared for are now musty targets of flooding, cursing their settled shoes. Carpets fear machines, matches fear sinks. Students fear heaven, with its small, cursive-covered stones.

Was there ever a divorce melee that didn't take our comforting horse out of the sky, the buckskin with the bran muffin kiss, and leave us with a potato substituting for a telephone? Not caring that heaven's a starved mountain, I set up my post office, lock the glass door.

# SUMMER'S GIFT CAKE

I was there when the world was cheap and useful, then I drank the pieces and fell to fighting with tides. Now each spring is a little more fallen, covered with milk, oil, and vegetable fat. It gets dirty gradually—by June it's a dusty road rising to bury the grass.

Talk to me. Tell me about that bread you're carrying: that familiar, dark baguette.

# SWIMMERS FULL OF SUNSHINE

Our old feathers are losing spiritual time, they're six minutes behind as of today. Who is the advertiser with the most to gain from this, from our poor decisions scattered like sand? In addition to the height of the dunes, we must again measure the size of the sand particles under which the fish are buried. We are always in danger of being too young, too tall and weak to scratch our names on the chosen shipwreck.

Sad to say, something whisked our diplomas from the piano's dark breast before the ceremony had bathed and shaved for our special day. But listen, in the middle of the book I'm reading, my hand is on your stomach, and a four-inch-tall horse invents games in the pool!

# TAPED TO A PIANO

We keep forgetting that classrooms are full of natural radios. When we remember, this awful cold wind stops and the German-made constellations take off and fold their tissue paper costumes. Fathers, don't ask how we improve the comfort of the forest with all its spirits!

It's an old machine that fills the sea. For the old people there are old microphones. The sound they make is B flat. The death rattle, which isn't really a rattle, is also B flat. Fifty-seven octaves below human hearing, a bell finding its voice first makes an insect sound.

# WHAT DREAMS LEARN ABOUT US

All night the road rises. Palm trees grow tall, fall down and grow back. We're nude, in a rush, stuck rummaging through boxes of single socks, ski hats, racks of nightgowns and huge sequined bras. Nothing even remotely fits or matches. Our abandoned responsibilities whistle so we hustle on, past hungry guests waiting at tables with no menus, no beverages, no utensils. It's understood we'll never manage to find them again, treat them well. Their sad eyes follow us. Each part of the city we see only once, our route a crumpled map.

The dreams cringe when we climb into cars—we are hopeless drivers, missing turns, launching off cliffs, driving into air. On foot we're worse, born lost, trespassing to find our way back. Just once we made a famous actor laugh in a supermarket—we seemed smart and prepared, for once. But the dreams tap their feet. They have no time to study either our many errors or what it is that we actually want as it all slides along under our steaming pillows. We sleep a lot, shocked and scared. We learn nothing that we can remember. The dreams lose patience. And now they're gone, our dear babysitter dreams, and they hid the door to their own real buildings, clouds, streets.

# WHAT JUST HAPPENED

In a closed room of the museum, evening, made of indigo lacquered paper, stepped with a delicate crunch on the pink sun's last moments. *It's not the artist's intention to preach to you,* the wall text read, *but winter is coming.* This place, this life—in a roundabout way, it belongs to you. As blood does, as bees do.

I tried making the most of limited space, living together the way history wanted us to. I was at least present when roll was called. I helped push. Eventually, however, my sad whistles of failure were hooted off the platform by the sound of an animal's hoof.

# THE WHOLE HORSE, NOT JUST THE HEAD

We arrived carrying a word we believed would grow. We believed that the number of such words was increasing. Get ready to be separated from your beliefs, said the desk clerk. After the pool freezes, the sun shines on.

Here's the truth about the warm breeze: it wasn't for us. We have memories, but they're as different as they can be. *You* only remember the locked pool gate, how the monsoon rains flooded your plans. *I* only recall finding a secret grass field that promised me a wardrobe of smoke. Okay, the 'dance' version of the hotel map failed to include the true distance from our bed, pink in the darkness, to our memory now of its damp masks pinned to the windows of the airport shuttle, an exact second image of us pinned to the sand, breathing our last.

# WHY THAT DARLING

I was green, innocent, I jumped into his arms. On our wedding day we fished solemnly for a monster-proof corner where we would sew clothes for the burned trees. Our newborn silence, which we swore was so good, broke a dish, releasing its gasp of farewell.

To be still long enough to photograph time is both a privilege and a constraint. Be patient, the land of ivory clouds comes closer with each coat-hanger smile. Now who will buy what's left of this shell, these mysteries of belief and bed? Wait, wait, our whales lift their heads right behind us, and though packed at sea after a life full of darkness, their silver garments (you didn't know?) are recycled into wonderful grooves.

# WINTER WHEAT

The farmer digs for puzzles below the surface of the ground. "The city of lavender's buried here," he says.

I confess to a certain amount of avoidance that starts in winter. There's nothing else to do in a room with such low ceilings, such an iron-hard floor where the grass used to be, so we sit down and wait. Once in a while a girl with red snow pants walks by, casting a James Turrell glow in the dimness. That's it. What more can happen to the dead? They have their mittens sewn on.

But actually it is the dead I'm most worried about. They have only their neuroses to get them through winter. How will we deal with that when we're also made of railroad ties dug up sentence by sentence? I'd just as soon we packed our sweaters, informed the city fathers, and ran away. What doesn't eat us first, feeds us.

I try to see on the calendar when our souls will reappear as a Gainsborough painting—the long robes, the crocuses, a glint of silver cup. Just because we didn't go until we did, the time still was, as always, suboptimal. (We stayed, we stayed, while muscular thighs ate the soil.)

I read in the thawing spring mud that your fortune took the train to the city wearing lavender sunglasses and was never seen again. In dreams our clothes hide from us. Why don't we leave before then?

# YOU CAN FINISH THIS WITHOUT ME

Remember, rivers are little machines for stealing. They are ready to drink up a large part of our money based on 'honesty first,' their language very warm and free. But oh, our wintertime mistakes are on the radio now, calmly and quietly, their honey flowing out.

Our name for the drink that leads us under the river is 'swimming lesson.' First it takes our confidential information and drinks it up. Our breath explodes into a hot and bloody silence, like a car driving with the smell of the moon's jacket left behind on the seats.

A little drink and we're ready to start. We have a lot of money, in a good way, at first.

# YOUR SPIDER KNOWS

The strict, bossy stars have no hands, just hooves or water pitchers or planets at the ends of their arms. They can't move us around by the head, make us quit a job or fall in love. But this little toy town they dreamed up—its petticoats are made of rabbit fencing, its rabbits big enough to ride to the store to pick up the starting over book.

## ACKNOWLEDGMENTS

"The Sitting Voice" and "Foreclosure Language" appeared in *Times Times 3*. "Inflight Meals" appeared in *Aperçus Quarterly*, "A Nervous Case of Family Romance" appeared in *Solo Voyage* and "You Can Finish This Without Me" appeared in *The Columbia Review*.

PHOTO **HOLADAY MASON**

**CELESTE GOYER** is a poet and visual artist living in Los Angeles, CA. She edited a literary quarterly for fourteen years and her poems have appeared in *Aperçus Quarterly*, *Scoundrel Time* and *The Columbia Review*, among others. Celeste is a member of the Wild Orchid Collective, based in Venice, CA, an interdisciplinary literary and visual arts group. Born in Northampton, Massachusetts, Celeste Goyer has lived in California since age 11, mostly in remote towns of the Mojave and Great Basin deserts.

www.ingramcontent.com/pod-product-compliance
Lightning Source LLC
LaVergne TN
LVHW040619250326
834688LV00035B/644